NUCLEAR ENERGY

To my children
Christopher and Andrea

Library of Congress Number: 82-9790

Printed and bound in the United States of America.

1234567890 8786858483

British Library Cataloguing in Publication Data

Coble, Charles
Nuclear energy. — (A Look inside book)
1. Atomic power — Juvenile literature
I. Title II. Series
621.48 TK9148

ISBN 0-86256-066-7

NUCLEAR ENERGY

By Charles Coble

CONTENTS

RB
Blackwell Raintree • Oxford

A NEW SOURCE OF ENERGY

Over the ages people have devised ways of doing more and more work by using energy beyond the strength of their own muscles. Societies that have used their sources of energy well have prospered.

During the last hundred years we have used much more energy than ever before. We have also changed our energy sources. At first, wood was the most commonly-used source of energy. Then it was overtaken by coal. Now oil and natural gas also give us large amounts of energy.

In the 1950s we began to use a new source of energy. This new source was more powerful than any source ever used before. It came from a very tiny particle of matter — the nucleus of an atom. At first it was called atomic energy, but we now also call it nuclear energy. Nuclear energy is the energy released by changes in the nucleus of an atom. In order to understand nuclear energy, you first have to know something about atoms.

ATOMS AND ELEMENTS

Atoms are the "building blocks" of all matter: solids, liquids and gases. There are 90 kinds of naturally occurring atoms. These atoms make up the 90 naturally occurring elements such as oxygen, carbon, iron, and so on. Scientists have made at least 14 other elements that do not occur naturally on Earth.

Atoms are made up of smaller particles called protons, neutrons and electrons. Protons are particles that have a positive electrical charge. Neutrons are particles with no electrical charge. Protons and neutrons make up the nucleus, the centre of the atom. Only one element is different: normal hydrogen atoms have only one proton and no neutrons in the nucleus.

The nucleus of every atom is surrounded by a "cloud" of electrons. Electrons are particles that have a negative electrical charge. The number of protons inside the nucleus is the same as the number of electrons outside the nucleus. Therefore, an atom is neutral; that is, it has a balanced electrical charge.

Each kind of atom has a certain number of protons in its nucleus. This number of protons is called the *atomic number.* For example, all atoms that have only one proton in the nucleus are hydrogen atoms. Thus, hydrogen atoms have an atomic number of 1. All atoms that have eight protons in the nucleus are oxygen atoms. The atomic number of oxygen is 8.

The nucleus holds almost all the *mass* of an atom. (Mass is a measure of how much matter is in an object.) The total number of protons and neutrons in an atom is called the *mass number* of that atom. For example, most oxygen atoms have eight protons and eight neutrons. Thus the mass number of oxygen is 16.

Although the number of protons in an atom of an element is always the same, the number of neutrons may vary. All carbon atoms have six protons. They

The carbon 14 isotope (above) has 6 protons and 8 neutrons in the nucleus. A normal carbon 12 atom (below) has 6 protons and 6 neutrons. Both atoms have 6 electrons.

usually have six neutrons. However, some carbon atoms have eight neutrons. Atoms that have the same number of protons, but different numbers of neutrons, are called *isotopes.* The most common form of carbon is carbon 12. It has six protons and six neutrons and therefore a mass number of 12. The isotope of carbon with eight neutrons would be called carbon 14, because its mass number would be 14 (six protons and eight neutrons).

Another element with isotopes is uranium. Uranium has an atomic number of 92, which is the number of protons in its nucleus. Two of its common isotopes are uranium 238 and uranium 235. Uranium 238 (U-238) has 146 neutrons. Uranium 235 (U-235) has 143 neutrons. The two isotopes of uranium play an important role in the story of nuclear energy.

RADIATION

Most atoms do not naturally change. They keep their original structure, with a fixed number of protons, neutrons and electrons. They do not normally release energy and light. They make up elements that are considered stable.

However, some elements are naturally unstable. For example, if you put a chunk of uranium on to a sheet of photographic film in the dark for several hours, it will "take its own picture". The film is exposed because uranium is unstable — it is *radioactive.* That is how radioactivity was discovered by the French scientist, Henri Becquerel, in 1896.

Radioactivity is a release of energy due to changes in the nuclei of atoms. (Nuclei is the plural of nucleus.) Radioactivity usually occurs in atoms heavier than lead. However, some of the isotopes of lighter elements are also radioactive. For example, certain isotopes of carbon and potassium are radioactive. You have a small amount of these

This is a uranium 235 atom. It has 92 protons, 143 neutrons and 92 electrons.

Diane Christensen

isotopes in your body.

Around the turn of the century Professor Ernest Rutherford (a New Zealander working in Britain) sent a beam of radiation from uranium toward a piece of photographic film. The beam was passed between the poles of a magnet. The magnet split the beam into three parts which made three spots on the film.

This and other studies showed that natural radiation is made up of three main types of particles called *alpha, beta,* and *gamma* radiation.

Alpha radiation is made up of positively-charged particles. Beta radiation is made up of negatively-charged particles, called beta particles. Gamma radiation is made up of waves of energy. Gamma rays are like X-rays.

Radiation can damage living cells and tissues. If the damage is bad enough it causes radiation sickness, which can be fatal. People working with radioactive elements have to be very careful. They must shield themselves and others from radiation.

Uranium and other radioactive elements can be detected with a tool called a Geiger counter. The invisible radiation sets off an electrical charge in the counter. This causes the counter to make a clicking sound. The amount of radioactivity is shown by a needle on the dial of the Geiger counter.

RADIOACTIVE DECAY AND HALF-LIFE

The French scientists Marie and Pierre Curie also studied uranium at the turn of the century. They discovered that the nuclei of some radioactive elements break apart. The breaking up of the nucleus is called *radioactive decay.* As elements undergo radioactive decay, they change into isotopes of other elements, which may also change. All radioactive elements give off gamma rays when they decay. Some also give off alpha particles, and some give off beta particles. Some radioactive elements give off all three.

Each type of radioactive material decays at a particular rate. A measurement of this time is called *half-life*. Half-life is the time it takes, on average, for half of the atoms in a radioactive material to decay. The half-life of uranium 238 is about 4.5 billion years. This means that in 4.5 billion years, 1 gram of uranium 238 decays to 0.5 gram. And it will take a further 4.5 billion years for that half gram to decay to a quarter gram, and so on.

The shorter the half-life of an element, the more radioactive the isotope. Some isotopes have a half-life of less than a millionth of a second!

It was the discovery of radioactivity that led scientists to achieve the amazing feat of splitting the nucleus of the atom and using its power.

UPI Photo

Marie Curie is shown in a photograph that was taken shortly before her death in 1934.

NUCLEAR ENERGY RELEASED

Albert Einstein (1879 - 1955)

In 1905 the great physicist Albert Einstein put forward a remarkable theory: that matter and energy were equivalent to each other. This meant that matter could be converted into energy. The amount of energy (E) produced would be equal to a given mass of matter (m) destroyed, multiplied by the speed of light (c) multiplied by itself (squared). His famous equation looks like this: $E = MC^2$

Einstein's equation explained why atoms — so small that half a million of them might be in the full stop at the end of this sentence — could explode into so much energy. His theory was proved in 1932, when a giant "atom-smasher" experiment released a tremendous burst of energy from a lithium atom.

In January 1939 German scientists discovered that they could split the nuclei of the atoms of uranium 235. The loss of mass was far greater than in any other previous atom-smashing experiment. The

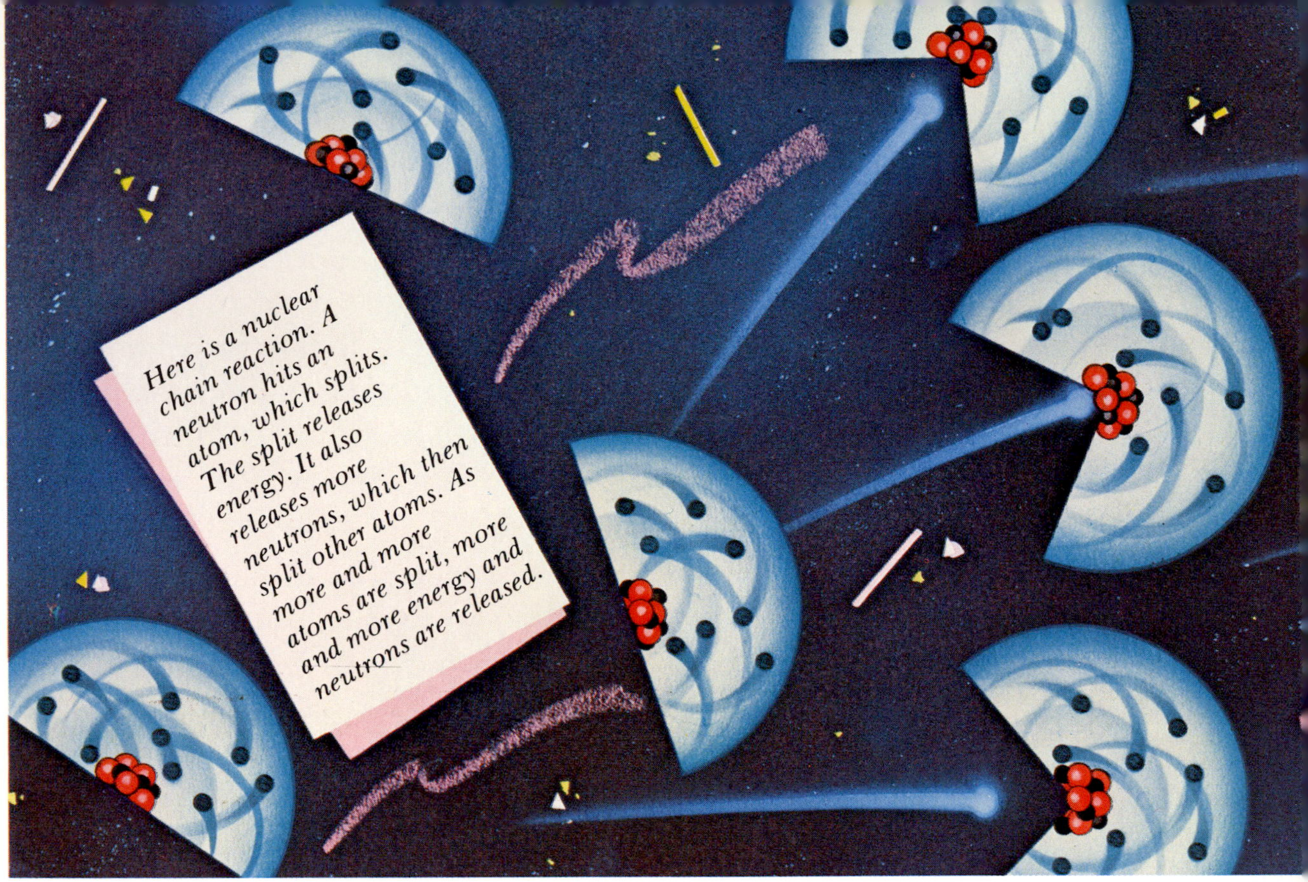
Here is a nuclear chain reaction. A neutron hits an atom, which splits. The split releases energy. It also releases more neutrons, which then split other atoms. As more and more atoms are split, more and more energy and neutrons are released.

splitting of the uranium also released an astounding amount of energy.

The splitting of atoms became known as *nuclear fission*. Fission means division. In nuclear fission one nucleus is split into two or more lighter nuclei. Those nuclei have less mass altogether than the original nucleus. The "lost" mass becomes energy in the form of heat and radiation.

Only certain radioactive isotopes, such as uranium 235, will split when struck by neutrons. During nuclear fission a neutron from one atom collides with the nucleus of a uranium 235 atom, causing it to split (fission). This releases other neutrons. These neutrons cause more uranium atoms to split, releasing still more neutrons, which may then split more uranium 235 nuclei, which free more neutrons.

The fission of nuclei and the release of neutrons goes on,

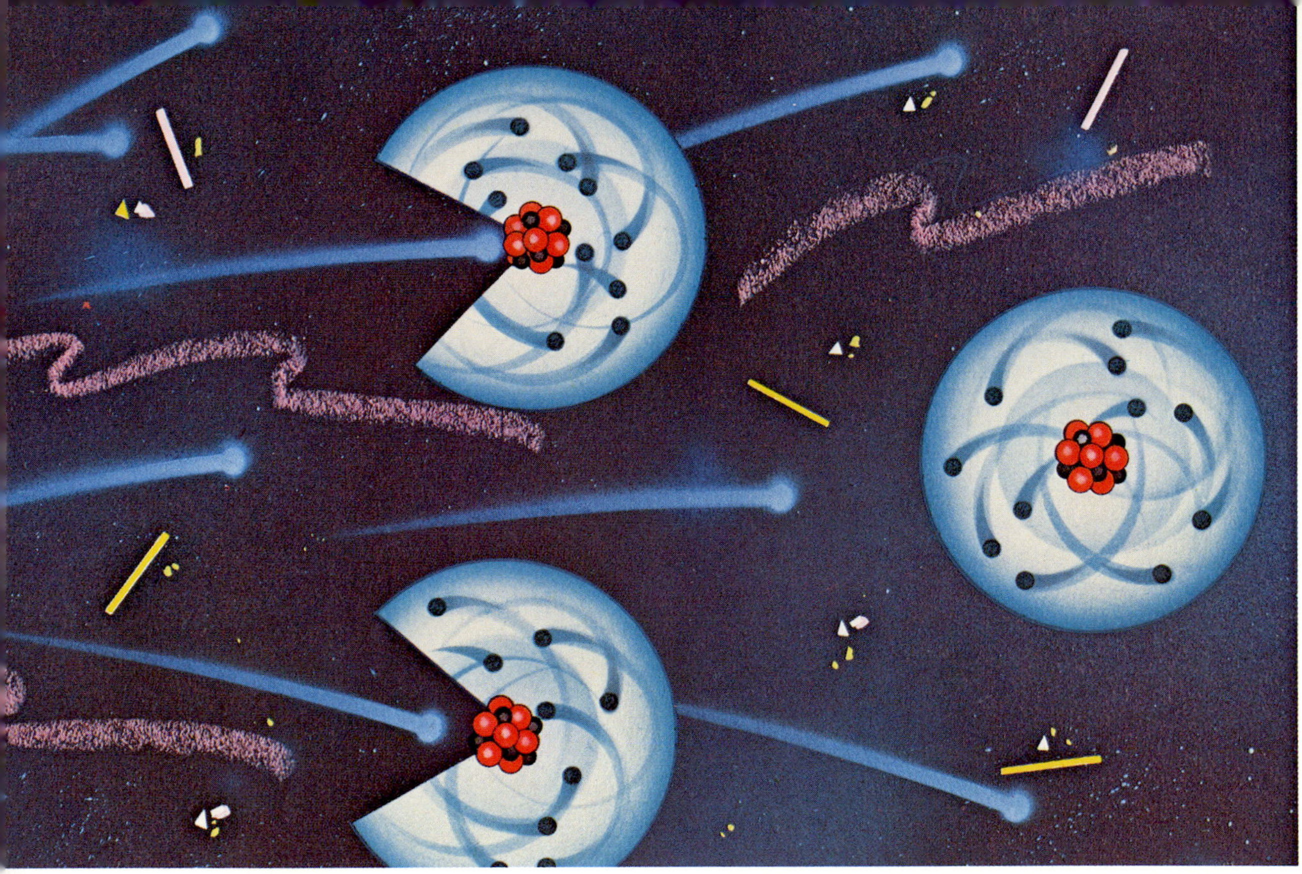
Diane Christensen

causing a *chain reaction*. A chain reaction is a series of events where one event makes the next one happen, which in turn makes the next one happen, and so on. A nuclear chain reaction can release a huge amount of energy.

Scientists in the United States who were studying fission realized that the energy released by a fission reaction could be developed into a weapon. These experiments were being carried out during the Second World War. The US government decided to put together a massive effort to develop a new weapon to help win the war against Germany and Japan.

The scientists knew that just the right amount, a "critical mass", of uranium 235 had to be present before a chain reaction could begin. The problem was to find out what that critical mass was.

They discovered that if pellets of uranium 235 were held in

blocks of graphite, they could more easily control the speed of the chain reaction. They began to build a pile of graphite blocks, some containing uranium 235. Cadmium rods were put into the pile. Cadmium is a metal that can absorb neutrons. Cadmium rods can stop a chain reaction and so could be used to control the experiment.

The pile was built at the University of Chicago. By 2 December 1942, the scientists had built about seven tons of uranium metal into the pile. As the cadmium rods were raised, the Geiger counters began to go wild, and heat began to build rapidly. All instruments showed that a chain reaction had begun. They immediately lowered the rods and stopped the reaction. For the first time, it was proved that energy from an atom could be released and controlled.

This painting shows the site at the University of Chicago where the first controlled chain reaction took place, in December 1942.

The world had entered the nuclear era.

The first use to which this knowlege was put was the building of the atomic bomb. Scientists worked out a way to load a bomb with a type of gun which shot half the critical mass of uranium into the other half.

The first atomic bomb was exploded in a controlled test on 16 July 1945, in the desert of south-eastern New Mexico. Only 21 days later, the United States dropped an atomic bomb on Hiroshima, Japan. The bomb had the power of 20,000 tons of dynamite. Nearly 100,000 people were killed in Hiroshima. Three days later a second atomic bomb was dropped on the naval base of Nagasaki, Japan. Five days later the Japanese surrendered.

The invention of the atomic bomb had enabled the war to be brought to a speedy end. But the effects of the bomb on its victims were devastating. It was clear that a terrible force had been released. It was also clear that that same force could be used as a vast new source of energy. So scientists began working to develop peaceful uses of atomic energy, in particular to produce electricity from nuclear fission.

By 1951 a small nuclear reactor was producing electricity in Idaho in the US. In 1956 the world's first commercial reactor came into operation at Calder Hall in England.

National Archives

Several days after two atomic bombs were dropped on Japan, World War II ended.

ELECTRICITY FROM FISSION

A nuclear power plant in California.

Most electricity is produced in power stations fuelled by coal, oil, or natural gas. These are called fossil fuels because they were made millions of years ago from the remains of plants and animals. In fossil fuel power plants, the fuel is burned to make heat. The heat is sent to a boiler to make steam, and the steam runs a turbine to produce electricity.

The reactor in a nuclear power plant does the same thing that a boiler does in a fossil fuel plant — it produces heat. The process that produces the heat is the splitting, or fissioning, of a radioactive fuel.

Uranium 235 is one fuel that can be used in a nuclear power plant. Pure uranium is a white metal more massive than lead. Rocks that hold uranium are fairly common.

However, the uranium in most rock is so thinly scattered that it is very hard to get out. The United States has about a quarter of the world's useful supply of uranium. It is found mainly in New Mexico, Wyoming, Colorado and Utah. Canada and Zaire also have large deposits.

Uranium is actually a mixture of the two isotopes U-238 and U-235. Only U-235 can be used directly for nuclear power. So the two isotopes have to be separated. Only a tiny fraction of natural uranium is U-235. The problem of sorting out U-235 from U-238 atoms is like finding and removing 7 good apples from 993 bad ones . . . except that it is even more difficult to do!

The uranium ore is first heated to a gas. Then the gas is given an electrical charge. Next, the electrically-charged gas is sent through a small hole between the poles of a powerful magnet. The magnet pulls at the atoms but the more massive U-238 atoms are not pulled quite as sharply as the atoms of U-235. The result is that the atoms separate and are collected into different areas.

There are other methods of separating U-238 and U-235. Almost all of them rely on the difference in mass of the two isotopes of uranium.

The core of the reactor contains the uranium fuel. A mixture of about 3 per cent U-235 and 97 per cent U-238 is formed into pellets. The pellets are about 13 millimetres (½ in) wide and 25 millimetres (1 in) long. They are stacked end-to-end in hollow tubes called fuel rods. The fuel rods are 3.5 – 4 metres (12 – 14 ft) long. The fuel rods are put together in bundles called fuel assemblies. About 200 fuel assemblies are then grouped together to make up the reactor core.

Some of the fuel assemblies contain control rods. They are made of materials which absorb neutrons, stopping them from splitting U-235 atoms. As the control rods are raised from the core the fission process speeds

On the right is an experimental nuclear reactor in the USSR.

Alpha Photo, Inc.

U.S. Department of Energy

Shown above is the core of an advanced test reactor (ATR).

up. When they are lowered into the core, the chain reaction slows down.

The fuel assemblies are arranged so that water or other cool liquids can flow between them. The liquid helps prevent the core from becoming too hot, and helps to control the fission process. If the neutrons which split an atom were going too fast, they would skip over the atoms and fission would not occur. Water slows neutrons down so fission can take place. If water were lost from a reactor by an accident, the chain reaction would stop. However, the reactor core could get very hot. This could release radioactivity into the air.

TYPES OF NUCLEAR REACTORS

There are various different designs of reactors, but they are all fuelled by rods containing uranium or plutonium. These rods are surrounded by a "moderator" (usually either water or graphite) which slows down the neutrons released by fission. The heat given off by the fission is carried away from the core by a coolant. Some reactors are cooled by water (either heavy or light). Some are cooled by gas. The most common type at the moment is the light-water-cooled reactor.

The heat produced by the

Atomic Energy of Canada Limited

Here are two nuclear generating stations in Pickering, Ontario, Canada.

reactor is used to produce steam which can then turn a generator to produce electricity — in just the way that steam drives turbines in an oil- or coal-fired power station.

Fast breeder reactors do not contain a moderator. They can produce more fuel than they use!

Nuclear energy was first used to generate electricity in 1951 at the Experimental Breeder Reactor in Idaho in the United States. Five years later Calder Hall, the world's first commercial reactor, came into operation in England. In 1954 the US Navy launched the first nuclear-powered submarine, the *Nautilus.* Modern nuclear-powered submarines can stay underwater much longer than the old diesel-powered submarines.

The amount of electricity

Alpha Photo, In

generated by nuclear energy grew rapidly during the 1960s and 70s. By 1978 there were more than 200 nuclear power plants in the world. About 12 per cent of Britain's electricity is made in nuclear power plants. World-wide, about 6 per cent of electricity is generated by nuclear power.

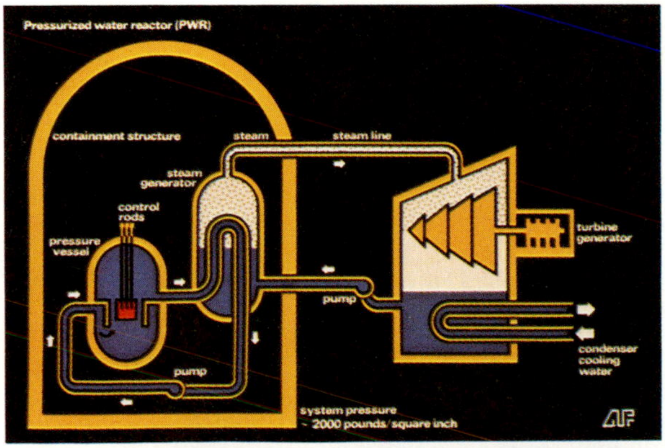

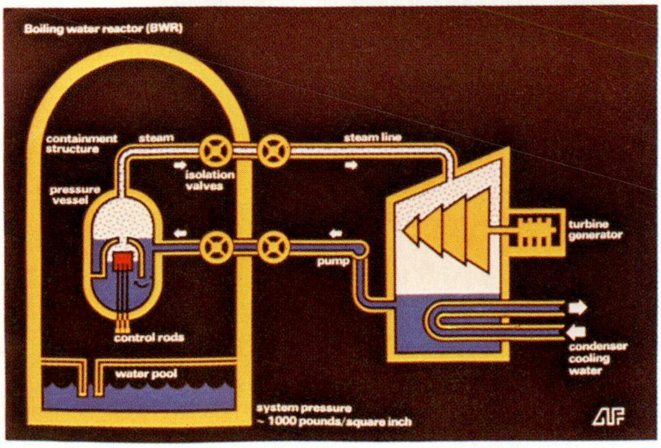

Atomic Industrial Forum

The photo on the left shows containment structures at a nuclear power plant. The diagrams above show two ways that steam can be produced in a nuclear power plant. In both cases, the steam runs a turbine, which in turn generates electricity.

NUCLEAR REACTOR SAFETY

The manipulator crane on the left is removing an assembly that contains used nuclear fuel. The used fuel will be stored at the nuclear power plant.

Many people fear nuclear power plants because they associate them with atomic bombs. However, U-235 in a nuclear reactor cannot reach critical mass and explode like a bomb. But the fission process in a reactor does produce radioactive materials which are extremely dangerous and some of them will remain dangerous for hundreds or even thousands of years.

Controls to prevent the release of this radioactivity are built into every nuclear power plant. Here are some of them:

1. The uranium is formed into ceramic pellets which seal in the radioactive material.
2. The fuel pellets are packed into special zirconium rods which also act as a barrier against the release of radioactivity.
3. The core is placed in a shielded steel reactor vessel about 20 centimetres (8 in) thick.
4. The reactor vessel is behind thick concrete walls.
5. All of these things are housed in an airtight building

made of steel-reinforced concrete about 1 metre (3 ft) thick.

6. An emergency core cooling system can pump thousands of gallons of reserve water into the reactor if the pressurized water supply drops.

7. The reactor is operated by remote controls from a central control room located in another building. In some reactors there is a second control room away from the plant for extra safety.

8. In addition to human workers, reactors have automatic controls. The controls will shut down the reactor when they detect a change from normal working conditions.

Westinghouse Corporation

The core of a nuclear reactor.

9. The second control room on new plants makes it possible to shut down reactors by hand from outside the central control room.

Unfortunately, safety systems are only as good as the people who build and run them. They can be turned off, and workers can make mistakes. These controls try to make up for that as much as possible.

Some low-level radioactivity is normally released into the environment. The amount of radiation from nuclear power plants is very low. You get more radiation from natural sources — in food, rock, soil, air and water. The average person in the US receives around 130 millirems of natural radiation a year. (A millirem is a unit of radiation exposure.) The additional exposure to people living within 80 kilometres (50 miles) of a nuclear power plant is less than 1 millirem per year. However, there are concerns about exposure to

S. Department of Energy

The technician above is using television monitors to inspect the fuel assembly in a nuclear power plant for defects such as deformation.

radiation from other aspects of nuclear power, such as mining the uranium and disposing of nuclear waste.

Two major accidents in nuclear power plants have also raised questions about their safety. The first major accident took place on 10 October 1957, in the Windscale nuclear reactor on the west coast of England. The reactor caught fire, and on 11 October was cooled with water. A

The Three Mile Island nuclear power plant in Middletown, Pennsylvania.

cloud of radioactive steam rose from the reactor and was carried by the wind over England, Belgium and other countries of Europe. No effects from this have been seen yet, but some scientists think that 10 to 20 people may die of cancer from this radiation by the year 2000.

Most people had forgotten about this accident by 28 March 1979, when several water pumps stopped working in the Unit 1 Nuclear Power Plant on Three Mile Island, near Harrisburg, Pennsylvania. In the minutes, hours and days that followed, a

UPI Photo

series of events involving equipment failure and human error resulted in a major accident. When the pumps stopped working, reactor coolant was lost. The core overheated, and the fuel was damaged. Some radioactive gases escaped. The reactor stopped working.

No one was injured or killed. The amount of radiation released was about one thousand times less than at the Windscale accident. However, many people were frightened by how easily the accident seemed to happen. Following the accident, the US President and Congress asked the

Nuclear Regulatory Commission to develop better safety procedures for nuclear power plants.

NUCLEAR WASTES

Though the burning of fossil fuels and nuclear fission are very different reactions, they both produce wastes. In a nuclear reactor, radioactive isotopes are created during fission. As these fission products begin to build up in the fuel rods, they absorb neutrons. This absorption slowly makes the reactor less efficient. Each year from a quarter to one-third of the fuel assemblies have to be replaced with fresh fuel. The used fuel is stored underwater in specially designed storage ponds. Some of the radioactive isotopes, such as hydrogen, strontium, iodine, and caesium, are very radioactive and are considered as high-level waste. Plutonium and unused uranium will also be left over from the fission process.

Some of the radioactive wastes of nuclear power plants have very short half-lives. They decay to stable, non-radioactive elements in seconds, minutes, hours, or days. A few, however, have very long half-lives and so have to be kept from entering the environment for a long time.

Radioactive strontium 90 and caesium 137 have half-lives of around 30 years. A small percentage of plutonium 239 is also present, but its half-life is over 24,000 years. These wastes have to be kept away from people and the environment for thousands of years. Plans have been proposed to store highly radioactive wastes in stable areas of land, like underground salt beds. Uranium and plutonium might also be re-used in nuclear plants. However, many people are worried about keeping these wastes safely for such a long time. They are afraid that dangerous radioactivity will escape. Added to this concern is the fact that plutonium could be used to develop nuclear weapons.

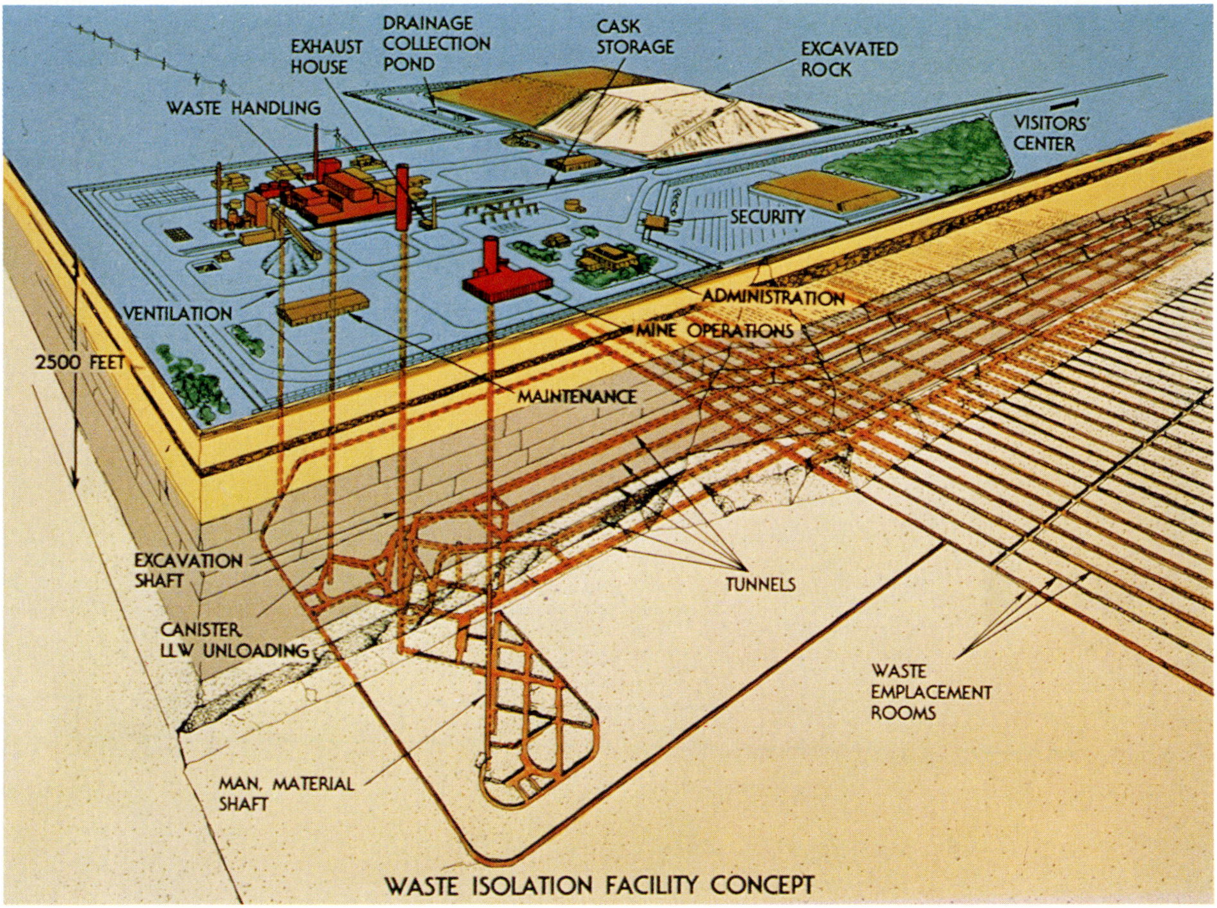
DRAINAGE COLLECTION POND
EXHAUST HOUSE
CASK STORAGE
EXCAVATED ROCK
WASTE HANDLING
VISITORS' CENTER
SECURITY
ADMINISTRATION
VENTILATION
MINE OPERATIONS
2500 FEET
MAINTENANCE
EXCAVATION SHAFT
TUNNELS
CANISTER LLW UNLOADING
WASTE EMPLACEMENT ROOMS
MAN, MATERIAL SHAFT
WASTE ISOLATION FACILITY CONCEPT

U.S. Department of Energy

This is a drawing of a National Waste Terminal Storage (NWTS) facility. The NWTS is a research project to develop a safe way to dispose of radioactive nuclear waste.

FUSION

This photograph of the sun was taken through a solar telescope from Skylab.

Another source of nuclear energy is nuclear fusion. Fusion means joining things together. In nuclear fusion two or more atomic nuclei unite to form a single nucleus and release energy. The energy from the sun comes from fusion reactions.

For nuclear fusion to occur, temperatures must reach millions of degrees Centigrade. The temperature inside the sun is about 15 million °C. This is hot enough for hydrogen nuclei to fuse, forming helium atoms. The helium atoms have about 1 per cent less mass than the hydrogen atoms. The lost mass becomes energy, in line with Einstein's equation, $E = MC^2$. About 25 million electron volts of energy are freed in the fusion of four hydrogen nuclei in the sun.

Scientists and engineers in many different countries are trying to control the energy released from nuclear fusion. However, it is still hard to do this. Two isotopes of hydrogen, deuterium and tritium, are the most practical fusion fuels. Deuterium can be taken from water. Tritium can be made from the element lithium. Deuterium and tritium can be fused to form helium and release energy. The energy could provide the heat to generate electricity in a fusion plant. The heat would be used to make steam to power a turbine generator.

Fusion needs very high temperatures. At these temperatures, in the millions of degrees, atoms are stripped of their electrons. Atoms as such no longer exist. This phase of matter is known as *plasma*. Plasma consists of nuclei and free electrons. If enough of the plasma can be held together long enough at the high temperature

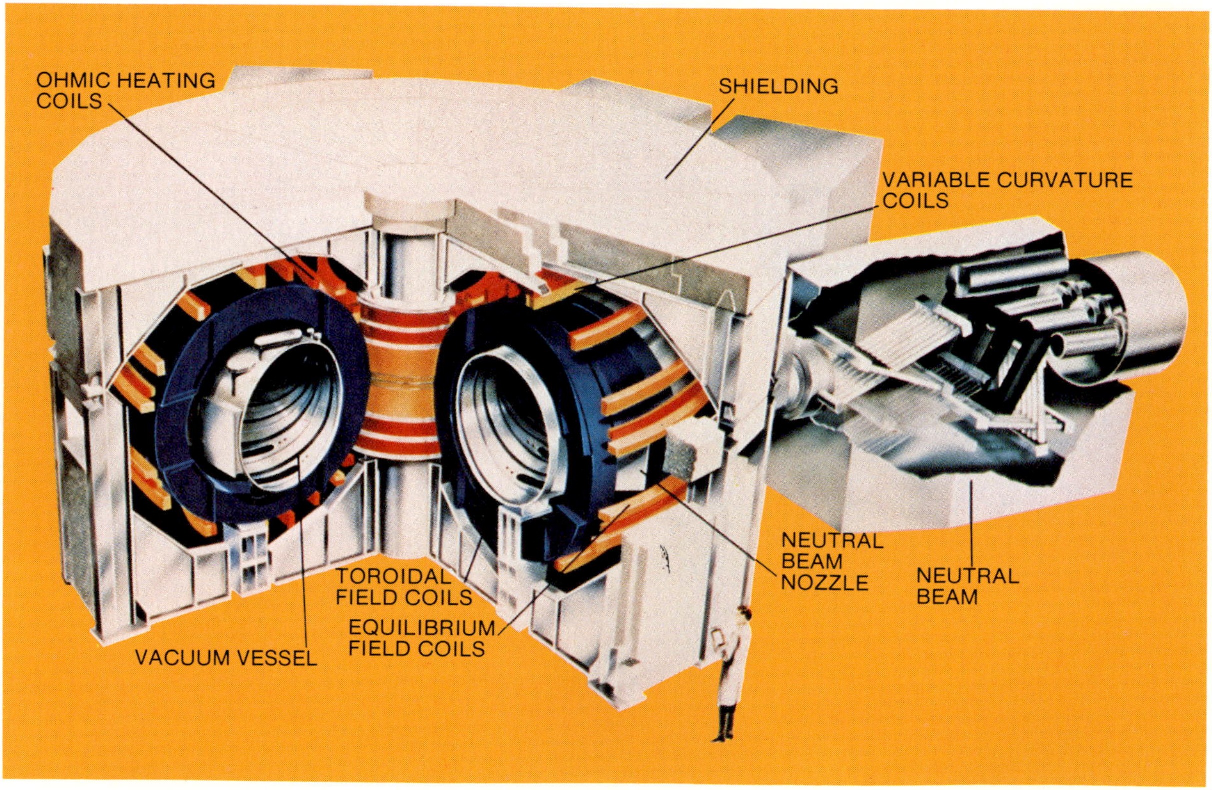
OHMIC HEATING COILS
SHIELDING
VARIABLE CURVATURE COILS
NEUTRAL BEAM NOZZLE
NEUTRAL BEAM
TOROIDAL FIELD COILS
EQUILIBRIUM FIELD COILS
VACUUM VESSEL

Princeton University

needed, the fuel will fuse to release vast amounts of energy.

The most promising method for achieving fusion power is in a machine called a *tokamak.* This doughnut-shaped reactor was developed in the USSR in the 1960s. Magnetic fields in a tokamak spin plasma in a circle. This allows the plasma to be held together very tightly, which is necessary for nuclear fusion.

Research into tokamak fusion test reactors is being carried out at Princeton University in the US and in the Atomic Energy Authority's laboratory at Culham in England. It is hoped that commercial fusion reactors might start generating electricity

On the left-hand page is an artist's drawing of a tokamak fusion test reactor. The photograph below shows a tokamak fusion test reactor.

Princeton University

between 2020 and 2030.

The fusion energy programme will be long and costly. However, the result would be an almost endless source of power, since energy could be taken from water.

Thermo means heat. Nuclear fusion is called a *thermonuclear reaction* because of the very high temperatures needed to produce fusion. The hydrogen bomb is a thermonuclear weapon. Thus, nuclear fusion occurs when a hydrogen bomb explodes. The temperature inside these powerful weapons is about 10 million degrees Centigrade. An atomic bomb is exploded inside the hydrogen bomb to produce the temperatures needed to start nuclear fusion. Once ignited, the thermonuclear reaction occurs in less than .000001 second.

Hydrogen bombs of almost unlimited power can be built. Both the United States and the Soviet Union have thousands of nuclear weapons. If the two nations used these weapons in a war, life on earth could cease to exist.

On the right is a photograph of a test explosion of a nuclear weapon.

U.S. Department of Energy

NO NUKES
IS
GÜÜD NUKES!

THE FUTURE OF NUCLEAR ENERGY

On the left is an anti-nuclear demonstration.

The future of nuclear energy is unclear. Concerns for safety, especially after the Three Mile Island accident, have slowed the development of nuclear power plants in the United States. The costs of building the plants have also risen dramatically. By late 1981, US plans to build new reactors had almost come to a halt.

In many other parts of the world, the use of nuclear energy is expanding rapidly. The UK, France and Japan are planning for nuclear power to provide most of their electricity in the future.

Research has shown ways to improve the efficiency of nuclear reactors. This will give us even more energy from fission. In addition, scientists and engineers have come up with ways to re-use some of the uranium 235 and plutonium that is mixed in with the nuclear waste. In the United States, recycling nuclear waste was forbidden by President Carter. He was afraid that dangerous plutonium could fall into the hands of terrorists, who might build bombs. However, President Reagan decided to allow recycling again, in hopes that this would help to make nuclear plants more efficient and cheaper.

Uranium is a rare element world-wide and only 7 out of every 1000 atoms of uranium can be used for fission in a nuclear reactor. These rare atoms are the isotope U-235. The more common U-238 is not readily fissionable. However, when "blanketed" around the core of a fast breeder reactor, U-238 can be changed into plutonium-239, which is more fissionable. Therefore, while the fast breeder reactor is generating electricity, it makes more fuel than it uses. In 12 to 15 years a breeder reactor could make enough plutonium to refuel itself and another reactor the same size. Experimental fast breeder reactors have been built in Britain, France, West Germany and the USSR. However, some people don't want breeder reactors to be built because they make plutonium. Plutonium is highly radioactive and can be used to build powerful bombs.

Useful energy from nuclear fusion is also possible in the future. As described earlier, enormous problems still have to be solved before it can be used to generate electricity. Yet, the abundant source of fuel (water) appears to make the effort worthwhile. In addition, fusion reactors don't make radioactive wastes, since nuclei don't break up as in the fission process. There would, therefore, be no worries about dangerous wastes.

In spite of all the problems and concerns with nuclear energy it remains a powerful and reliable source of energy. What do you think about nuclear energy? Do the benefits of nuclear energy outweigh the problems? Should we develop fast breeder reactors? Our answer to the question of nuclear power may decide the quality of our lives.

The photograph below is of a reactor that is used to test nuclear fuel and components for irradiation—exposure to radiation. The reactor containment building, in the centre, is surrounded by dump heat exchangers. Samples of nuclear fuels and other materials are placed in the core to determine their reaction to being exposed to radiation.

U.S. Department of Energy

This map of the world shows the concentration of commercial nuclear power plants that had been completed or were under construction in the early 1980s.

GLOSSARY

These words are defined the way they are used in the book.

alpha particle a positively-charged particle given out by an atom during radioactive decay

atom the basic part of all matter; the smallest part of an element that has all the chemical properties of that element

atomic number the number of protons in the nucleus of an atom. All atoms of an element have the same atomic number

beta particle a negatively-charged particle given out by an atom during radioactive decay

coolant a fluid used to cool a nuclear reactor and carry heat. It also moderates, or slows down, the fissioning of neutrons

critical mass the smallest amount of fuel necessary to sustain a chain reaction

deuterium a form of hydrogen that is twice as heavy as normal hydrogen

electron a basic particle that orbits the nucleus of an atom and has a negative charge

fission the splitting or breaking apart of a heavy atom into two or more new atoms

fusion the joining of two or more atomic nuclei to form one nucleus and release energy

gamma ray a form of high-energy radiation given out by the nucleus of an atom

isotopes different forms of the same chemical element which have different numbers of neutrons in the nucleus

mass number the sum of the protons and neutrons in the nucleus of an atom

millirem a basic unit of radiation exposure

neutron an uncharged particle in the nucleus of an atom

nucleus the core or center of an atom, containing protons and, usually, neutrons

plasma a collection of charged atomic particles

radioactivity the property that some elements, such as uranium, have of giving out alpha, beta, or gamma rays

tokamak a doughnut-shaped device that holds plasma tightly together in a fusion reactor

turbine an engine powered by spinning blades

uranium a heavy radioactive element, the basic fuel of many nuclear reactors

INDEX